# PLATFORM PAPERS

QUARTERLY ESSAYS ON THE PERFORMING ARTS
FROM CURRENCY HOUSE

No. 56
August 2018

CURRENCY HOUSE

# Platform Papers Partners

We acknowledge with gratitude our Partners in continuing support of Platform Papers and its mission to widen understanding of performing arts practice and encourage change when it is needed:

Neil Armfield, AO
Anita Luca Belgiorno-Nettis Foundation
Andrew Bovell
Jan Bowen, AM
Jane Bridge
Katharine Brisbane, AM
Elizabeth Butcher, AM
Penny Chapman
Robert Connolly
Dr Peter Cooke, AM
Sally Crawford
Wesley Enoch
Ian Enright
Ferrier Hodgson
Larry Galbraith
Tony Grierson
Wayne Harrison, AM
Campbell Hudson
Lindy Hume
Professors Bruce King and Denise Bradley, AC
Justice François Kunc
Dr Richard Letts, AM
Peter Lowry, OAM and Carolyn Lowry, OAM
David Marr
Helen O'Neil
Martin Portus
Lesley Power
Professor William Purcell
Queensland Performing Arts Centre Trust
Geoffrey Rush, AC
Seaborn Broughton Walford Foundation
Caroline Sharpen, Creative Industries Consulting
Sky Foundation
Dr Merilyn Sleigh
Maisy Stapleton
Augusta Supple
Christopher Tooher
Caroline Verge
Rachel Ward, AM and Bryan Brown, AM
Kim Williams, AM
Professor Di Yerbury, AM

And we welcome our MAJOR CORPORATE SPONSOR FOR 2018

To them and to all subscribers and Friends of Currency House we extend our grateful thanks.

# Platform Papers Readers' Forum

Readers' responses to our previous essays are posted on our website. Contributions to the conversation (250 to 2000 words) may be emailed to info@currencyhouse.org.au. The Editor welcomes opinion and criticism in the interest of healthy debate but reserves the right to monitor where necessary.

Platform Papers, quarterly essays on the performing arts, is published every February, May, August and November and is available through bookshops, by subscription and online in paper or electronic version. For details see our website at www.currencyhouse.org.au.

# FALLING THROUGH THE GAPS:

## Our artists' health and welfare

MARK R.W. WILLIAMS

# ABOUT THE AUTHOR

DR MARK WILLIAMS practises in Melbourne as a solicitor in copyright and the law as it pertains to the creative sector. He is also an Adjunct Professor in the School of Art at RMIT University. In his words, he is a product of the Melbourne University theatre circuit including the Law Revue from 1977. As part of the naissance of the Melbourne comedy scene, he wrote, performed and directed whilst graduating in Arts-Law and undertaking articles of clerkship. He then headed to Oxford University where he performed in as much student theatre as was consistent with completing a DPhil, which turned out to be a substantial contribution to the knowledge of how theatre of the 1610s and 20s actually worked on stage. Ten years followed earning half a living from the theatre.

After seven years as a partner in a Melbourne firm of lawyers, he has been in sole practice since 2003. He has advised large, medium and small performing arts companies, appeared in tribunals, instructed in the courts and lobbied for performing arts wages and conditions on both sides of the fence. He has also worked for over twenty years negotiating venue contracts for the big stage musicals on behalf of Melbourne's major lyric theatres. He has been at the forefront of copyright convergence issues including Federal and High Court cases on copyright infringement and the protection of confidential information. This has included work for film, television, computer games, music, stage and visual arts organisations.

Other theatrical activities include being drama critic, for mainstage and later fringe, for PBS-FM 1990–2010, and President of Melbourne's annual Green Room Awards, of which he now holds a Life Membership. He has served on the board and later as chair of Melbourne's Bharatam Dance Company (1986–2000), has been a board member of Arts Access Inc., Viscopy Limited and Currency House, and is now with Polyglot Theatre and the Committee of the Victorian Actors' Benevolent Trust.

# Acknowledgements

Thanks to, and sometimes despite, the best efforts of the NBN, I have been able to wade through the minutes of actors' welfare organisations of the 1870s; to thumb through the trust deed for the New York Philharmonic Pension Fund for 1944; I have travelled, virtually, to Milan and to St Petersburg; details of leave loadings and residuals from the past do not need to be retrieved from storage; pieces of folklore and anecdote can be readily checked and, in some cases, verified.

But Google isn't nearly enough. It has been people and their deep knowledge that has been integral to this project. My thanks to many associates, colleagues and friends who made suggestions or gave me links to the many and varied resources referred to here on a subject I thought would not be nearly so hidden from view, and which are so vital to developing the case set out here.

I would particularly like to thank: Dr John Adamson, Founder, Camerata Musica, Cambridge, UK; Robyn Arthur, VABT and MEAA; Dr Colin Benjamin OAM; Louise Connor (formerly MEAA and Media Super); Susan Cooper, General Manager, Entertainment Assist; Blair Edgar OAM; Matt Emond, VABT and City of Greater Bendigo Councillor; Professor David Forrest, RMIT University; Richard Hobson; Jacques

Hughes; Derek Latham; Jeanette Liddell; Dina Mann, VABT; Ken Marshman, Trustee VABT; Dr Katya Petatskaya; Clare Pickering, Archivist, VABT; Simon Plant; Mark Rowe, General Manager, Her Majesty's Theatre, Melbourne; Frank van Straten AM; Sioban Tuke, VABT; Sally-Anne Upton, President VABT; Janet Watson and Katharine Brisbane, the Editorial Committee and the readers at Currency House for accepting the proposal and for their rigorous editing and positive, challenging comments.

Above all, I thank my wife, Fiona Gruber, for all her insights going back to a cast list for *The School for Scandal* in the 1770s containing RB Sheridan's notes on her British ancestor's acting role: 'scratch Groves'; and another Groves—Fred, who worked for Fred Karno's circus and developed the silly walk that Charles Chaplin took over when Fred Groves left the company. Many giants stand on the shoulders of pygmies. Then there was the BBC radio star of the 1920s, Olive Groves and her orchestra. One great regret is that I never met her uncle, the actor and English Equity stalwart Donald Groves, who died a week before he was due to move into the UK retirement home for performers, Denville Hall. He was the last of the Groves, now an almost forgotten theatrical line stretching back at least to the 'scratch Groves' annotation.

To the Groves family: you aren't forgotten.

# Prologue

If you are lucky enough to enter the actors' bar on a 'Thirsty Thursday' after a happy show has just come down, the atmosphere is fantastic. We're in Her Majesty's Theatre, Melbourne. The noise levels are far higher in the confined space than in the house. The cast have performed three shows and have five more to do that week. Cast and crew, wiggies, dressers, sound techs, mechs and flypersons, chorus and stars, are in that happy egalitarian space we think of as Australian theatre. They are talking at the tops of their voices, the room is full of physical beauty, they are confident of their skills and, even if the majority is being paid award wage and no more, the house discounts the drinks and has turned on food. Some will be staying in one of the luxury hotels that like to be known for catering to show business, others will be trying to save what they can of their per diems by staying with good friends and renewing intense friendships from drama school. When the run is over—in six weeks, or thirteen or, maybe, with luck, two years on the road—they'll be unemployed and may never see one another again. Some may be in the business for another forty years. Most won't be.

Because what is written of here relates to incomes and welfare, the independently verifiable evidence would have been impossible to gather in any other age. These are private matters in a profession where people are expected repeatedly to come up smiling no matter how relatively well or badly they are treated. All the same, there are limitations: not everyone has detailed, searchable archives; Australian companies had and still have a regrettable tendency to destroy financial records as soon as they can after seven years; and a lot of people still ain't sayin'. Without the discussions with many members of the professional theatre and a lot of work in my own career assisting producers, performers, managers and policymakers, the hunches would never have been had and the questions and searches could never have taken place.

Some years ago an international cabaret performer I know was told by a sensible Australian aunt: 'All you'll have at the end of it all is a scrapbook and some memories.' It was meant with some animus (or as a spur to bourgeois acquisition of material things). In Aesop's fable of the Grasshopper and the Ants the ant diligently toils at ground level whilst the grasshopper blows in the breeze leaping from stem to stem; but in the winter, it is the ant that huddles up safe underground ready to emerge and do it all again. What the fable failed to acknowledge was that the grasshopper's life, though short, was a brilliant one and his descendants would be there again next summer.

Economists like David Throsby, and the Nobel Prize winner, William Baumol, have pointed out that the concept of financial reward in the arts can be seen quite differently from that of pecuniary reward; but its economy has rules that can be used for analysis and prediction. One of those insights is that, in many cases, performers and other artists gain considerable psychic reward and, except in the case of superstars, forego pecuniary reward in pursuit of it.[1]

Economics has much more to say about life choices than just the choices that maximise cash rewards. Even the Australian Taxation Office agreed some years ago in the Pedley case that an artist might be 'in business,' despite a poor income; and commented wryly in another that whether the taxpayer had 'a purpose of profit', a 'prospect of profit', from the activity, constituted a problem for the taxpayer.[2] And then there's health. After that, we might look at what else a person needs on Maslow's hierarchy of needs. If self-actualisation sits at the top, and making and working with great works of art brings one toward it, some seekers will always struggle up to grasp it before they have a firm footing.

So, keeping the prize firmly in view, let's have a look at the base of Maslow's pyramid for workers in the performing arts. At the welfare level, there are terrible dangers of falling through the gaps between psychic satisfaction and material security in their career path. My argument, based on a ten-year period earning half a living as an actor and thirty years as a lawyer, is that these gaps are structural. They need fixing.

Here goes.

# 1. The Issue

So how did we get here? Whether it's Allen Ginsberg's, 'I saw the best minds of my generation …', or some other lament going back before Menander to the effect that 'those whom the gods love die young', we do lose a great number of our storytellers far too early and forever. We also know many living down inner-city lanes or in places no better than squats. Some are with their aged parents in small country towns on quarter-acres, or out in the bush with dubious plumbing. Some are in hostels or homeless. We lose a noticeable number, predominantly men aged in their fifties, to suicide, substance abuse and related cancers. In the last twelve months they have been designers and directors—a surprise possibly because those tend to be roles in the theatre where some longevity is possible. These are relatively high-profile figures in stage or screen but are personally known only to a few in tight-knit communities. They have died, often in squalor.

Lex Marinos described the jobbing actor in his Platform Paper last year (*The Jobbing Actor*, PP53) as the person who actually does manage to make a life-long career in the performing arts. It is the thesis of this paper that the same conditions that have allowed the general standard of living in Australia to rise for ordinary working people have failed the ordinary working actor and other members of the professional performing arts community. One respondent to my challenge quoted the late Gordon Chater's advice from fifty years ago: 'Spend a third, invest a third and never touch the rest.'[3] Perhaps, just perhaps, that is better advice now than it has been for fifty years.

This is the core issue. The problem is how to:

- call out the stereotypes;
- alleviate the risks associated with financial insecurity, mental and physical health issues and adverse family circumstances;
- bring the standard of living of those working in the profession up to the standards of the community in 2018;
- address problems of savings, whether for retirement or a rainy day; and
- overcome the barriers to keeping a roof over one's head.

# 2. The problem

For those who do not have a family member or ancestor in the business, perceptions of the actor's lot can be largely divided between substantial fame and wealth on one side and penury on the other. In former decades it included people cast out from community by race, sexual preference, accident or, indeed, freakish ability. Some made good, more didn't. Now we call out what used to be elided as a third category of unlovely or unlikeable figures cast aside: alcoholics, substance abusers, the mentally exhausted; the bitter and twisted. To these we might add yet another category of once-successful leading men—and others in positions of power—disgraced after decades of sexual predation.

These categories also describe many other professions; the distinction is that those performing artists who have achieved great heights and made substantial contributions to our culture and society will, by comparison with the rest of working Australia, still end up poorer, have worse mental and physical health, and a shorter lifespan. And the traditional support networks—the family, charity, the welfare state or free-market economics—will have failed them. That means, as a society, we have failed them. We have failed ourselves.

In the light of the recent, highly publicised accusations

of sexual misconduct it is worth stressing here that none of us condone criminal behaviour. In stage and screen performance the expectation of just deserts is inevitably a moral element; but I prefer here to adopt the Salvation Army motto, 'Love the sinner: hate the sin.' Crime, or even sin, is *not* involved in a very great number of careers that end in poverty and neglect.

In short, this paper is about people brought low for all sorts of reasons. A disproportionate problem for members of the performing arts is that, unless they are hard-headed about making the most of their 'brand' they are likely to be poor and to have poor health.

The structure we have is so full of gaps that it cannot properly support professionals in the performing arts at a level compared even to other citizens with equivalent training and talent.

One of the surprises, in researching this paper, was that the first thing the American Actors' Fund did after its foundation in 1882 was to buy *burial* plots in New Jersey. The stigma attached to actors was such that they were not even given a decent burial.[4] It was an actor who shot Abraham Lincoln in April 1865. People remembered. The North-American public of Puritan origin that had just endured a Civil War was a tough audience before whom to make a case for the welfare of actors. London had had its own 'Actor's Acre', now part of Brookwood Cemetery, since 1857, where 'leading members of the profession should lie side by side with those of similar importance'.[5]

The theatre will be the model here because I know it best. As its lawyer I know pretty much where every cent of the price of a theatre ticket goes. Film, television and the *revenue* models of the digital platforms I find far more opaque. My colleagues who do work in these areas tend to agree. How the revenue is divided is always complicated by the costs of capital and infrastructure, long lead times and global markets. Music business also has its unique characteristics when it comes to revenue and remuneration but studies in the Appendix suggest that the structural problems are similar. The theatre too is far from dead as a source of employment or audience activity: big stage musicals cost as much per hour to mount as most Australian feature films or television series; and a small fortune in weekly running costs; but their economics work very nicely when they play in houses of 1,200 to 1,800 seats, to 85-100 per cent capacity, eight shows a week for thirteen or 26 weeks. State theatre companies in Melbourne and Sydney attract audiences of 15,000 to 20,000 per production but run longer initial seasons than Australian films. By my calculation cinematic releases of feature films with Australian or shared Australian creative control averaged *national* audiences of 85,500 per film between 2013 and 2017—though having only one or two hits per year makes it harder to calculate the modal figure.[6] The touring circuits nationally and internationally also provide opportunities and audiences. The flesh and blood theatre is far from a spent force.

But few actors, writers, voice artists, directors, or

designers make careers in Australia just from the theatre. On the way through, we also talk about dancers, opera singers, variety performers, circus artists, musicians; and we always keep crew in mind. The working conditions and remuneration models for such workers have the same features as the live spoken-word or musical theatre—and opportunities trickle down from the film studios, television production houses, digital platforms and so on.

Theatre, then, is the model for this discussion, but when it comes to consideration of remuneration and reward—monetary or psychic, career path and career structure—there is plenty applicable to workers at the coalface of all performing arts. Some of it might even apply to the rest of the 'gig economy'.

Dancer Jeanette Liddell, who toured with JC Williamson's Theatres in the 1950s, subsequently recalled being the only white member of the African-American Katherine Dunham Company which passed through Australia and into the Pacific and Asia around 1964. The experience completely transformed her life, artistically and politically, she says. But on the tour she could afford a diet of only fruit and milk and had to pay for her own stage make-up. She returned to Australia weighing four and a half stone.[7] Later she worked twelve to fourteen hours a day learning choreography, and performed live most nights as one of the Channel 9 dancers on Melbourne evening television. Eventually she completed a master's degree in physical education with specific reference to the Dunham method. Dunham's work in introducing African dance to American theatre was continued in the Alvin Ailey American Dance Theatre and left a significant legacy in Australia. Melbourne practitioner Blair Edgar, OAM, travelled in the 1960s to London, where he performed as both dancer and actor, and provides further contrast:

> *In London I earned £28 per week, but when I got to New York, the fee was US$1,000. Out of that $1,000, I paid US tax, UK tax, my agent took ten per cent of the first week and I had to pay my dresser. I also paid ten per cent to US Equity.*[8]

My point here, and task, is not to make value judgments but to point out that fifty years ago, on Broadway at least, separate provision was made at source for performers' welfare and is still the case today. By contrast, any such tradition in the Australian system was shaken out of the industrial fabric last century and now rests on the Superannuation Guarantee Charge (SGC)—of which a little more later.

# Incomes, health, welfare and housing

## Incomes

The previous examples might seem to have been plucked from an insider's Facebook page, but empirical support comes from David Throsby and Katya Petatskaya's findings in *Making Art Work,* published in November 2017.[9] The population of Australia's artists has aged significantly in the last five years with 41 per cent aged 55 and over in 2016, compared to 32 per cent in 2009 and up from only 17 per cent in 1988. Note that this is a figure for all artists, visual and performing and includes musicians.

The most obvious thing to be said about this is that performance is predominantly regarded as a young person's game. As a profession it has many reasons for this. As an industry, theatre has a great deal of trouble valuing the experience that comes with age. A chorus or corps de ballet role is a chorus role whether you have been dancing for forty years or are moonlighting from drama school. In some traditions such as Russian Ballet, Chinese Opera or Japanese theatre these roles are achieved only after years of training. In our more cost-conscious western tradition a performer can achieve the illusion of age without the imperative to give it respect. A career as a performer will also involve touring and sacrifices of family life.

How to pay the experienced performer for roles that are required tends to be resolved by setting a basic rate—in effect setting experience at naught economically. Industrially, there are some bonuses for experience built into the various performing arts and film and television awards, but any such differential will always push the cost-conscious producer to economise on experience over compliance. What the singer-songwriter Jackson Browne once described as 'the energy of the innocent'.[10]

The statistics in David Throsby and Anita Zednik's 2010 study, *Do You Really Expect to Get Paid?* also bear out the general sense that conventional employment is being ousted by the gig economy. In Throsby and Petatskaya's 2017 study, the proportion of actors' and directors' earnings from freelance activity is 57 per cent, up from around 43 per cent in Throsby and Zednik's 2010 study.[11] Figures are similar for choreographers and dancers: the proportion of freelance income in 2017, at 68 per cent, is up from 56 per cent in 2010. Musicians and composers in 2017 are both shown as earning 86 per cent of their income from freelancing where, in 2010, musicians earned 67 per cent and composers earned 97 per cent as freelancers.[12] All of these amounts relate to income from Performing Arts Occupation (as defined), not from more general income sources. Apart from the smaller contingent of composers, the figures demonstrate that there is a very substantial decline in income from PAYG wages in the period. The interval happens to encompass the aftermath of the Global Financial Crisis of 2007–8. The specific causes of these rises and falls in the performing arts are more difficult to ascertain.

## Long-tail Income

Artists in general have also had rights to participate in schemes to deliver additional income through copyright royalties and residual payments. This is not the place to go deep into the argument that every performer should hold a copyright in recorded performance . Some people say it's a form of compensation, others that it is a fundamental human right to receive reward each time their work is used or enjoyed. My rationale is that at the time work is made, no one knows how to price it.

A blindingly good recorded performance, composition, manuscript or even picture may take a generation or more to achieve its audience. As a matter of justice and economics, treating the price of a play as 'ten per cent of whatever you get' is far more equitable than fixing a lump sum which may be too high for a producer to pay or far too low. On that theory, long-tail income is simply a pricing mechanism. It certainly isn't 'money for nothing'. The problem is that, as we see profit for the record industry come back from a near-death experience after a decade of piracy and unremunerated file sharing, actors and other performers may not be in the race.

Throsby and Petatskaya's report comments that indirect earnings as a proportion of artists' incomes in all art forms tend to be rising, particularly from copyright revenues and revenues from the Education and Public Lending Right (ELR and PLR) schemes; but for actors and directors, five per cent is still not a high proportion of income.[13] In the earlier equivalent study by Throsby and Zednik, the relevant table lists actors (but not directors) as receiving only three per cent of their income from royalties and advances.[14] As might be expected, only writers and composers receive a substantial proportion of their income from royalties and advances: 20 per cent and 21 per cent respectively in 2009; 27 per cent and 16 per cent respectively in 2014–15.[15]

'Long-tail' income is something in which I have a professional interest, having been a copyright lawyer for most of my working life and had the benefit of serving on the Board of the Visual Arts Copyright Collecting Society (Viscopy). Viscopy was subsumed into the much larger Copyright Agency in mid-2017 and the latter administers what is likely to be a growing source of long-tail income for visual artists, the Resale Royalty: five per cent on every public sale of an artist's artwork from the second sale in the public market until the expiry of the copyright—a lifetime plus seventy years.

I also spent time a few years ago looking at the fate of the 1989 provisions in the Copyright Act which gave performers' rights in the quaintly named 'fixations' of their performances for up to 25 years.[16] It's important to stress that this did not change the payment structure of the live performer one jot unless a cast recording or video was being made; and further enhancements of rights through the Australia-US Free Trade Agreement created complex rules without achieving real benefit for performers other than, perhaps, musicians and singers.[17] We found that after performers gained these rights, in the event of a cast recording they were bargained into a higher fee. These rights were recorded in the Actors' Theatrical Award while video or residual royalties were enshrined in the Actors' Film and Television Award—a small percentage of what was known as the Basic Negotiated Fee or BNF. In practice, even that turned out not to be as good as it sounded; and for nearly twenty years performers were badly short-changed. Film and television production companies in Australia didn't count for much in the tax maelstrom created for the benefit of investors, at least until the advent of the producer's offset in 2007. They regularly folded or were reduced to shells after production was complete and, if their records didn't disappear on the way, they did as soon as the seven-year record-keeping provision required by the Tax Act expired.

What would you and your family prefer? Market price at the time your work was sold, then five per cent every time your work changed hands for the rest of your life plus 70 years (the current term of copyright), as is the case for visual artists? Or, as in the present case of the recorded performance, a reducing percentage of the basic negotiated fee, which expires after four broadcasts, and which could be enforced for a maximum of only

25 years from the date the performance was recorded? In the case of members of an orchestra, opera or ballet company, at the time the performance is recorded for transmission, these rights are negotiated and artists usually paid a loading, while some might also earn residuals. It depends on the initial broadcast contract.

In thirty years of copyright's wrestle with the performing arts, Australian film and television writers maybe gained something—performers, no. Meanwhile in the booming art market, visual artists were brought into some sort of parity with systems which had been in place in continental Europe for a century.

Then there is the long-tail income which the general public might associate with fame. It's an odd proposition to be known for the rest of your life for a role you played in your teens, twenties or thirties—and you may well have been paid very poorly for it at the time. Indeed, it may have been a role in an advertisement or a campaign of commercials. Other figures and personalities also received residuals, but in the epoch of strong bargaining for television rights in enterprises outside television drama they were often paid quite well. What fat is left in the long tail of early fame can be important, but is it bankable?

## Health

Look on the company noticeboard backstage during the run of any big show in a big theatre. Apart from rehearsal schedules and, sometimes, the dread notice that a show is to close prematurely, the board is usually covered with phone numbers and cards for doctors, dentists, physiotherapists and allied health professionals. Casts and crews have been drawn from all over the country and are often far from their home bases. Contacts to professionals who are available at short notice, and are familiar with injuries and the imperatives of performance, are essential. A notice board, even when it moves to a company website, answers a more regrettable need: it can be checked quickly and discreetly.

The content of a company's notice board reveals two key factors that cause members to fall through the gaps in the supposedly universal health system: high mobility and the need for discretion during a time of peak performance. Compared to the fevered discussion every week throughout Australia of the problems with this or that sportsperson's ACL, shoulder or groin, the health of a dancer, acrobat or performer is rarely of concern to the wider public—and that's when people are in work. What resources are available for those who aren't? The image conjured up by an inaugural meeting of roadies (touring cast and crew) in the first phase of the Entertainment Assist/Victoria University study on performers' health, is vivid:

> *... the St Kilda gathering had hearing problems, injuries to their backs, feet and shoulders, and he stated: 'It was a dentist's nightmare. I've never seen so many missing teeth in one room in my life.*[18]

What this and the final report showed was that working

irregular hours correlated with sleep disorders and insomnia; and that this in turn showed connection to mental health disorders, including severe anxiety and depression, suicidal ideation almost nine times greater than the general population and suicide attempts more than double. The statistics from the Executive Summary are so shocking—and were said to be a world first when they were published in October 2016—they are reproduced in the Appendix. Again, in discussions with actors regarding this paper, bad teeth were mentioned by several as a feature among them, mostly products of pre- or post-fluoridisation generations. They are also an Australian indicator of relative poverty.

## Mental Health

Of the factors such as broken sleep, disconnected social support and related compensatory reliance on substances to the point of substance abuse, another factor that the academic literature has noticed but which has not leaked out into the wider world[19] has implications for all of us: personal competition and perfectionism can be toxic. Doing something unique or specialised to the height of human (or even our own) ability creates a curious paradox in the quest for psychic support. The very people who might 'get' what you are on about are your competitors, striving to reach heights that, by definition, no one else can attain.

There is also a psychic toll-taking in being before the gaze of producers, casting directors, fellow artists, the public and the critics, all of whom hold aspects of your fate in their hands. Others are stressed by having one or more colleagues or managers in their lives to whom they must report. The performer, even some of the most experienced—Sir Anthony Hopkins was one publicised instance—can find playing other people becoming far too stressful. Sir Anthony may have been able to afford not to work for a few years. Most cannot.

To perfectionism, which afflicts many professions where the day-to-day standard is nothing less than optimal performance and competitive pressure, I would add another feature which perhaps is more pronounced in the performing arts: separatism.

## Separatism

By this I mean the separation from 'normal' society of the performer who works irregular hours and the self-imposed separation of celebrity, applied to achieve privacy; and also the separation of being a minority by race or gender, someone other than the general population. John Hargreaves, the quintessential model of the knockabout Australian actor, who died in 1996 of an AIDS-related illness at 50, left a rare insight into the causes of the depression that plagues so many creative people, in this quotation from a posthumous biography:

> *When you're making a film, you sort of become this huge instant family [...] you tend to become very close while you're making the film. You seem to*

> *know people terribly well [. . .] you seem to get terribly close to people. But the day after the shoot finishes, everybody vanishes and goes their separate ways, and you may never see these people again. You may not even want to. So where is the reality in that?...*
>
> *In fact, you haven't become close at all. You've been as close as a family, by necessity, for the film. So you do it [. . .] I have the feeling that in my life I've been on a train that's hurtling through the countryside. And every now and then I pass a lighted window, and there's a family in there, and I see a life going on [. . .] but I'm not part of it. I'm observing it. I think for a lot of actors that's very true.*[20]

No statistic for prevalence of people who would identify themselves as LGBTQI has been attempted in the Australia Council studies. Despite certain public perceptions, the professional theatre, in the view of production and company managers, and my own observation, seems to track, on average, around the same as the general population for same-sex attracted people. Perhaps more people in the theatre have been *out* for a long time but discussions with a wide circle across different generations tended to support my perception. The relevance lies not in current issues of discrimination but has been highly relevant in the past and is also relevant to our identifying what gaps still occur in a community where LGBTQI people are supported and celebrated.

On the separate question of family size, the demographic analysis from the 2017 Throsby-Petatskaya study shows that the proportion of all actors/directors and dancers/choreographers who list themselves as single tracks roughly the same: 34 per cent actors/directors, 35 per cent dancers/choreographers and 37 per cent of musicians (the figures for writers, 20 per cent and composers, 24 per cent are revealing) against 31 per cent for the general labour force; 28 per cent, 36 per cent, 41 per cent respectively as married or partnered with no dependent children, which could include those whose children have left home (writers 49 per cent, composers 46 per cent again provide contrast), against the general population's 34 per cent. Eight per cent of actors/directors list themselves as single with dependent children, double the figure for the other categories of artist.[21] The significance of these choices is again hard to establish here. Are performers a little more likely to be single or childless than the general working population because of what they do or who they are?

It's enough for this purpose to say that with fewer children to care for, those works in the performing arts are about 20 per cent more likely to be on John Hargreaves's speeding train than inside the conventional home.

## Gender

The theatre is again a stand-out in the Throsby-Petatskaya report when it comes to gender balance: the proportion of male actors and directors is far higher—61 per cent. In most other art forms and roles measured in this survey, the proportion of women is far higher, which brings the total average closer to 50-50 across the sector. Writers, in particular, swing the balance the other way with women making up 65 per cent, second only to women who comprise 69 per cent of dancers and choreographers.[22]

That's probably where the good news ends. Apart from dancers and choreographers, men feel established in their careers earlier than women, see no discrimination on the basis of gender and do not feel that caring for children holds their careers back. For women the reverse is true.[23] Men continue to gross more than women and women are severely under-represented at annual income levels over $50,000. The real significance is that these gaps are cumulative. Despite acknowledgement that the gap is narrowing, gender imbalance means that, particularly for those who are single, there are fewer opportunities to support their art, afford housing or gain financial security in older age. Women artists (not restricted to performers) tend to live more in regional and rural Australia, which offers reduced living costs but poorer access to services.[24]

Another pachyderm in the playground is that self-employment means no paid maternity leave. Theatre companies no longer maintain permanent ensembles under long-term employment contracts. In the last state theatre company to do so, the Sydney Theatre Actors' Company (2004–07) two out of the five women members of the twelve-strong company took maternity leave in the first year of a five-year program, later cut to three years.[25] Within the national companies Australian Ballet and Opera Australia, there is more room to accommodate. For everyone else contemplating having children, they are on their own when it comes to industry support.

## Ethnicity

The calls made in other Platform Papers, and in the wider theatre community, for the performing arts to embrace a more representative diversity of Australians, have their correlation in the Australia Council studies. The proportion of practising professional artists born in Australia is 87–94 per cent across the performing arts categories—far higher than that of the general population at 70 per cent. Only ten per cent of artists come from non-English speaking backgrounds (NESB) compared with 18 per cent of the general population.[26] There is a very low incidence of artists with Asian backgrounds.[27] People with African backgrounds have no statistical presence. We will speak of Indigenous Australians later.

This cultural time-lag may be corrected, with or without the active intervention of existing managements and funding bodies, but in a curious reversal, there are today many ageing members of the performing arts community who are doubly invisible because they derive from tiny minorities in the whiter Australia of the past. Second-generation Australians from communities which have later become multicultural, may never know the courage of the first non-Anglo actors, singers, dancers or backstage participants who pioneered their way into a more mainstream acceptance. That recognition ought to be something the profession does for its members. It is another reason to search out, celebrate and support their past leaders.

## Life Expectancy

Figures quoted in the Entertainment Assist/Victoria University 2016 report for the music industry are particularly stark. In the US, figures show that life expectancy for musicians over the period is *on average* 25 years shorter than that of the general US population. Death from suicide or the effects of drugs and alcohol is particularly pronounced, beginning several years after retirement or decline in popularity.[28] This study is far from perfect as the total population of musicians was not objectively measured and the figures were drawn from notices or obituaries in the music press. By contrast, my lifespan calculations were drawn from the lists prepared by Frank van Straten for the Green Room Awards, for 434 theatre professionals who died in the years 2003–13. The mean lifespan was 74.88 years. The lives measured comprised those cut short by cancer, suicide or accident and three who died aged over 100.[29] The average life expectancy at 20 for the Australian population is currently 84 for men and 89 for women; but whether working in the theatre makes for a shorter life-span of this magnitude would require a great deal more work to draw a national picture.

Another thing to bear in mind is that half the sample is greater than the mean. In the headlines about short life-expectancies, we must not forget the other danger: longer lives in relative ill-health and reduced economic circumstances. It is at this end point we must remember with gratitude the Actors' Benevolent Funds and Trusts around the country which have for at least sixty years been providing assistance for people too poor to pay for their own funerals.

## Housing

Around 1990, at one Melbourne Festival, I was asked to read the translations of a celebrated visiting actor-poet before he delivered his originals in Bahasa. The artist's name was Rendra. He managed to make a living on the festival circuit, not just for himself but for his theatre company. The reason he did so, he explained, was because of the political climate at home in Indonesia. President Suharto had taken exception to his company's work, imprisoned him for nine months in 1979 and banned the company's work from then until 1986. During the ban their response was, in Rendra's words to me, 'to buy land and to make our work'. Whilst prohibited from performing, Bengkel Teater had been able to raise families and sustain itself, not as an institution, but at the fundamental level of a community of artists. Rendra died in 2009. He had been repeatedly nominated for, but never won, the Nobel Prize for Literature.

Can you imagine any Australian company adopting such a response to censorship and the withdrawal of all political and social support? Only those with nothing left to lose. Certainly not those dependent on grants or other subsidy, whatever the political climate; probably not even those with the *price* of a house; possibly not even those with an inalienable right to their land. Compare this with the careers of the small but significant number of Indigenous performers in Australia. They pay a terrible toll if separated from country by the demands of the artistic life but many of our most significant do have a community and country to return to between performances. Whatever your hierarchy of needs may be, housing is fundamental to artistic freedom. It is fundamental to *cultural* freedom whether or not to cultural autonomy.

This issue of housing is particularly acute for the Australian performer who needs to work across a massively decentralised cultural scene. In the 1960s, to quote playwright and Pram Factory centre-halfback John Romeril, the Australian Performing Group at the Pram Factory in Carlton (1970-80) only had 'ten pay packets' at the core of a company that not only created a localised Australian theatre in Carlton but largely stayed there until Carlton itself changed its demography.

In the 1970s and 80s performers had to be prepared to appear regularly for work in Sydney, Melbourne, Brisbane or Adelaide; by the end of the 90s they were soloists or duos—almost never more than quartets—touring their own shows to the other capitals and every festival town in between; then up into Singapore and Kuala Lumpur, Osaka and Seoul, New Zealand and Nandi and cruise boats across the Pacific. *Plus ça change*, perhaps, when one looks at the touring companies over the previous generations; but *ça* has changed: the big choruses have become rare; productions are smaller—with limited casts, recorded music, minimal lighting and computer-generated effects, lower travel costs, sets and costumes compact—and fees not much more than the minimum wage plus a per diem for the cast and crew, without regard to the sunk cost of production development, advertising and reputation building.[30] The same is true of opera, dance, music theatre, spoken-word theatre and even film, television, games development and live music. Careers have to be mobile, nimble, without much bag or baggage: potentially, nowhere to call home.

The consequence of mobility is deracination. The statistics, though, are not easy to find. Performers in work are paid per diems and other living away from home allowances under the Live Performance Award; and agents and managements negotiate payments. Standards of accommodation at the 'legitimate' end of the market are part of the normal contract process with the relevant awards underpinning those figures. Meanwhile, there are small tours, profit-share and not-for-profit productions where life out of a wheelie suitcase is far more informal. What we don't know is whether these performers on the road continue to pay rent, pay mortgages or, in the case of some I know, buy houses or flats during periods of relative income stability. Some have even been able to sell in a rising market, cover the incidental costs and keep enough equity to go back into the housing market when steady work, like a long-term tour or television series, comes around again.

# 4. How did we get to this?

Somewhere in the nineteenth century, the model of the actor manager, touring a circuit with a small company of players in much the same way as travelling fairs or circuses moved from town to village to farm, had become standard. Patterns developed over decades and modified as small villages grew into large manufacturing towns, boom towns in the goldfields merged back into the bush, cities developed from trading ports or concessions. These companies often centred around two or more generations of the same family with a mixture of other couples, with or without children, single men and apprentices. Whilst single women were engaged in such companies they often found marriage to a member of the company the best protection against accusations of scandal.

In the Australian context, the pioneering careers of merchant Barnett Levey, who founded Sydney's Theatre Royal in the 1830s and comedian-entrepreneur George Coppin, who came out to Australia in 1843, show considerable continuity from English models. Coppin's methods of managing both his theatre companies and his theatrical enterprises included a rigid hierarchy, hard work, constant travel and, the expectation that the next success was around the corner.

'For the Benefit of Mr/Miss [Insert name here]' could solve a financial emergency and was also the time-honoured method of placating a disgruntled actor by advertising a performance that would highlight the performer's talents and earn them a share of the profits: 'My dear boy', or girl as the case may be, 'I'll give you a ben', and the complainant would be placated with the thought of their name at the top of the bill and a crowded house that would fill an empty purse.[31]

These were the days before substantial income tax. Today the tax system would discriminate severely against any such practice. The benefit concerts or performances which occur these days are usually for a single purpose like overseas training, establishing a community facility; or for the benefit of families of the suddenly deceased. These can usually only be tax effective where the funds raised are lodged with a not-for-profit charitable entity, usually a trust.

Even then, one of the many lessons I have learned over thirty years associated with both commercial and not-for profit production and related activities, is that the hope of saving someone's fortune, let alone the proverbial orphanage, by putting on a show, have been crippled by the fixed costs of production. The minutes of organisations hopefully planning a benefit and receiving substantial sums (as was the case, for example, with benefits for the Victorian Actors' Fund [later Trust] at its foundation in 1958) show great profit and low overheads gradually whittling away to losses. Venue and catering charges ate into any reasonable returns on effort. By the 1980s or 90s the idea of the benefit was dead.

The English models withered too. The Actors' Benevolent Fund in England ceased benefit performances in 1914 and only revived them in the late 1980s for a brief period. The stand-out benefit is the Royal Variety Performance which, with Royal patronage and television rights, continues to be a vital support for performers' charities.[32] This reality, however, does not stop performers being called upon to give away their performances for the benefit of others. Whether they see it as enlightened self-interest or true altruism, performers collectively are better at looking after others than they are at looking after themselves.

At least until the First World War, the Distressed Actors' Fund supported actors and their families who were unable to work through illness or other disability and was associated with the Australasian Dramatic and Musical Association.[33] A few relics survive from this time of well-organised benefits, including a costume football match and fête in Melbourne, said to have been adopted also for Sydney, plus other benefit concerts at Melbourne's Princess Theatre.[34] Apart from more conventional sickness benefits, the funds also contributed to rescuing casts stranded up-country after the failure of a producer or closure of a tour.

Whatever tradition there may have been of structured philanthropic or benevolent support from Australian theatre producers for performers or crews passed to the performers' union, and the Actors' and Announcers' Equity of Australia (now the Media, Entertainment and Arts Alliance, or MEAA). J.C.Williamson Theatres (JCW) dominated the Australasian theatre scene from its inception in 1879 until the mid-1960s and finally folded in 1978. Before the First World War, JCW ran substantial benefits programs for members of their opera, variety and comic opera companies, eligible after six months' service and providing benefits available when a member was off work for a minimum of three days.[35]

By the end of World War Two the picture had changed. There was nothing by way of a pension or other funds, performers from the 1950s and sixties have assured me. 'We were grateful for the work. Getting taken on by Willamson's generally meant a tour of two to three years.' Derek Latham, a production accountant with JCW, in the period until the company closed, was equally clear that there were no deductions or salary sacrifices made to any benevolent fund or other pension system for production workers or permanent staff of the company. This came after introduction of the Whitlam Government reforms (1972–75) which included the 17.5 per cent loading for holiday pay.

Accounting was done weekly by production. Staff overhead costs were 20.5 per cent: ten per cent of which was an allowance for holiday pay, five per cent payroll tax, four per cent workers' compensation and 1.5 per cent long-service leave provision. One benefit was that casuals who worked more than four shows a week were also entitled to two weeks' pay at the equivalent of six shows per week after a year's employment; but Derek comments that he cannot recall anyone ever being paid long-service leave.[36]

The Tivoli Circuit was not so democratic. A document from 1956, retrieved from the ruins of the Tivoli Theatre in Melbourne, contains a list of the Tivoli employees entitled to participate in a proposed staff superannuation plan. The general manager was to be rewarded handsomely on retirement, with benefits extending down to the office staff; but no performer, whether on stage or in the pit, is mentioned, not even the conductors or designers for the company.

This is relevant today because the situation then is still affecting the welfare of those aged in their late seventies and early eighties, who have lived on the age-pension for ten or more years, but still consider themselves performers and regularly work, or hold themselves out for work, in the theatre. Paradoxically, the whole point of the Benevolent Funds was not about the creation of a retirement safety net but a safety net for those who were still active, but unable to work through illness or other hardship.

Another levy known as the Industry Service Fee (ISF), managed by Live Performance Australia (LPA), still applies to cover support from LPA in the event of industrial action.[37] Once upon a time levies were also payable to an MEAA fund to support cast and crew when a show failed. This seems to have disappeared from the Performers' Collective Agreement and may well have been deleted when the Howard Government safety-net provisions, first known as the Employee Entitlements Scheme, first heaved over the horizon in 2000, then transformed into the General Employment and Entitlement Scheme (GEERS) from 2001, and then, from 2012, as the Fair Entitlements Guarantee (FEG).[38] The problem with all of them, of course, for the performance sector, was that they applied only to employees in permanent employment. They do not address the problem of unemployment, under-employment or hardship or where the applicant has not had the opportunity to build up individual savings.

## Working hours and conditions

One big change, however, is in the efficiencies available to film, television and, to a lesser extent, theatre rehearsal and shooting scheduling. Where once actors might have lounged on a feature film location for weeks or sometimes months before their scene is shot, or supporting actors or chorus would be scheduled for shooting as their scenes came up in sequence, software now enables labour to be planned down to the minute, the three-hour call, or other fractions of the day or night.

This too has its downside. Early in my discussions, various actors said words to this effect:

> *I'm a household name and recognised internationally, thanks to my regular appearance over several series on television or for up to twenty years in a regular role. I might not be in every episode but I will be in running story lines. My character has grown up, been promoted, developed a back story but, at most, it amounts to two weeks' work.*

> *Sometimes all my scenes will be shot in one day. I'm scratching for work the other fifty weeks of the year. When people tell me my reputation has never been higher, I'll tell them my bank balance has never been lower.*[39]

The point is not to re-hash the plot of *Singin' in the Rain* or the more recent Oscar-winning *The Artist*, in which one actor is put out to pasture by the advent of new technology. What I *am* saying is that there will always be casualties of technological change. What we have seen since the advent of free-to-air television, slow as it was to arrive in Australia, is that yet another generation of performers is approaching poverty; but this time it is occurring even whilst their services are still firmly in demand. All other costs have grown and in-built 'cost disease' continues to apply to theatrical content.[40] In reality, performers have absorbed the pressure to offer their day-to-day services for less and less. This is not just less and less money, it is also fewer working hours and longer working lives eking out smaller rewards.

No sole-trader actor can afford to let their brand slip into obscurity by declaring themselves to be unemployed or retired; but the reality in Australia is that, no matter what unique skills, experience, awards and honours a professional performer may hold by mid or late career, most are underemployed or spend long periods 'resting', developing new work or, indeed, waiting to get paid for jobs. All of these factors are treated individually by the industrial relations: tax, social security and arts-funding mechanisms. The problem has been recognised for well over a generation but no one has yet been able to harmonise the systems.[41] In the following section, whilst my concentration is on actors, most other workers in artistic pursuits—and many another freelancer—face similar structural problems: their reality does not conform to those of the nominal Australian workforce.

## Industrial Relations

At the centre of the way actors are engaged is an idiosyncrasy which, to my lawyer's eye reveals a long-standing structural ambiguity. The Live Performance Award and the Actors' (Theatrical) Award which preceded it and the equivalent film and television awards, contain the apparently innocuous requirement that an individual contract be entered with each performer. The contract includes minimum provisions such as identification of the length of engagement, breakdown into rehearsals and performances and so on, which reflect variables not covered by the award. Other industrial awards don't need to do this. Short-term 'contracts'—even though the relationship is one of employment in the professional theatre—is a structural assumption. Many actors' tasks are not mentioned in the contract or in the award at all, such as the time required to learn parts, pre-production meetings with directors and designers and myriad other criteria which are left to 'the custom of the industry': arrangements with agents or individual house style. The reality is that, even when employed, actors are on their own in a way that is quite different from employees in steady employment in other industries. The structural ambiguity reflects the fact that an unambiguous employment relationship is far from the norm for actors and other freelancers working in the performing arts. This flows through to ambiguities in taxation and eligibility for grants and other support from government, but the first problem confronting most workers in the performing arts in between engagements is the need to seek income support.

Governments of all persuasions seek to reduce the official unemployment statistics. Most research that I am aware of stresses that gainful employment is better than no employment for health, mental health and, of course, the bank balance. Our present unemployment benefit system is directed to those goals. It has become progressively more difficult to mesh freelance work and the intermittent opportunities of the performing arts with such a regime.

# 5. Industry-based institutions

Australian institutions do exist to support performers, crews and other creative contributors to the performing arts. The Actors' Benevolent Fund in NSW was founded in 1944.[42] The NSW fund states that its original purpose had been to support the wartime welfare of actors and their families whilst the principal breadwinner was on military service. The Fund appears to have been national in intent. The Victorian chapter of Actors' and Announcers' Equity of Australia (now Media, Entertainment and Arts Alliance or MEAA) were unable to gain registration with the Victorian Charities for the purposes of making similar public appeals.[43] After the war, the Victorian Fund was formalised following a series of fundraising activities. These included benefit performances by visiting English artists from 1958 and with guidance from the equivalent English funds. A formal trust deed was executed in 1963. From 1975, the Actors' and Entertainers' Benevolent Fund of Queensland has also fulfilled a similar role in that state,[44] whilst the funds in South Australia and Western Australia have a less formal structure and role. The remaining states and territories tend to be looked after by the older bodies. There are also close connections to the equivalent fund in New Zealand.

These funds, broadly speaking, began in the post-war era through industrial organisation under the auspices of Equity. For individuals to apply or be nominated for assistance, union membership or, at least former affiliation, was required. Contributions to the fund were voluntary, in that the funds operated as mutual self-help funds provided by those who could, contributing both for the benefit of themselves and for others less fortunate. With the dismantling of compulsory unionism during the early part of the 1990s and from 1992 the introduction of Superannuation Guarantee Contributions, the funds responded by dropping the requirement for union membership. Identification with the profession is now largely the only criterion for assistance and crews are now also eligible.

The NSW fund in particular benefited after its foundation from several large bequests, including one half of the royalties from the plays of Nick Enright (1950–2003). The Victorian fund has an endowment built up from its early fundraising activities and subsequent contributions from voluntary pay deductions. Income is augmented by bucket rattles after a curtain speech by cast members (the old nineteenth-century model again), bequests, and ad hoc donations in memoriam or when prompted by notices in the industry press.

Each of these benevolent funds operate on principles similar to the English and other international models, in that they are for the relief of immediate hardship and are no substitute for pensions or other regular income support, health benefits or other forms of state assistance. Requests are considered in strict confidence and are sometimes made on behalf of a nominated person, who is often too conflicted to ask for assistance. A regular response is one of relief tinged with regret at the need to have asked because there are others worse off.

One feature, however, that first became significant during the AIDS crisis of the 1980s and 90s is that assistance may sometimes include support to obtain diagnoses or tests from specialist authorities still not supported by Medicare; or for drug treatments not yet listed on the Australian Pharmaceutical Benefits Scheme. Backed on occasion by expert opinion, participation in subsidised trials or for not-yet-approved medication involves sometimes quite substantial outlays—and there have been some almost miraculous recoveries based on otherwise unobtainable diagnoses or access to courses of expensive, non-subsidised medications.

In the music business, the latest addition to the picture, Support Act, was founded in 1997.[45] It is directed towards the welfare of music industry participants and is not connected with the union. Its support comes through the copyright collecting societies, APRA, AMCOS, PPCA, and from the Australian Recording Industry Association, ARIA. For all the challenges faced by the copyright system, the long-tail benefits of copyright for composers and recording artists represent income streams largely denied to live performing artists.

Other funds and organisations each tackle different

issues associated with health, welfare and professional development. The Equity Foundation, which now sits separately from the MEAA trade union structure, was established in 2002 and has the role of assisting actors' professional development. The Australian Major Performing Arts Group also convened Out from Under in September 2015 to address the stigma of mental health issues. Entertainment Assist, which includes board representation from MEAA, states it is committed to reducing the 'shockingly high rates of anxiety, depression, suicide, isolation and other matters associated with working in the Australian entertainment industry'.[46] The 2016 study and report quoted earlier has not only raised awareness but brought about considerable change and ripple effects internationally, particularly in Britain. Some of those ripples have led, among other initiatives, to the Performing Arts Wellbeing Summit held at the Sydney Opera House in November 2017

## Centrelink

Access to social security payments is a recurrent theme in the debate about artists' incomes in general and actors in particular. Whatever 'the dole' is named during any political cycle, eligibility criteria sit very, very badly with how professionals in the performing arts make their livelihood. Whether actors, to use the flagship example, are self-employed, serially employed or unemployed, the Centrelink provisions continue to apply more and more difficult compliance criteria, particularly with regard to income declarations for both the individual and any partner. As support to the jobbing actor, Centrelink is inappropriate: it is not a pension or a support system for the arts industry. It is specifically a social security fund to enable the unemployed to find work. Centrelink actively encourages people to re-train. To put it another way, the system actively discourages people from remaining in their chosen profession as part of the bargain for entering the social welfare system.

Using May 2018 figures, the maximum fortnightly payment for a single person is $545.80.[47] NewStart allowance reduces to nil once a single person's income reaches $1,053.34 per fortnight. Separate rules allow a single homeowner up to $253,750 in other assets before becoming ineligible for benefits or $457,750 if they do not own a home (and the bewildering 'granny flat' interest provisions don't apply). One is allowed to earn up to $104 per fortnight without affecting benefits. More importantly, rental assistance, health care and other supports also kick in. Likewise the slightly higher aged pension is available to those over 65 with similar levels of assets to NewStart; and the individual is still permitted up to $168.00 of paid work per fortnight. For a surprising number of household names the dole or the age-pension provides essential support. Again, more research would need to be done to gain effective statistical evidence for a very common discussion among mid- to late-career actors.

## Tax

The Australian income tax system works extremely efficiently when collecting money from employees and other service providers under the Pay As You Go (PAYG) system. But in the case of working actors whose work is well paid but comes in short bursts, it is a danger. Income averaging for the really big year is intended to allow the highly successful some measure of protection from a progressive taxation system[48]—and I use 'progressive' in the technical sense that the tax burden gets proportionately higher the more you earn. But this has little or no benefit to the freelancer who is trying to hold enough money in hand each fortnight to pay the basics and stave off the unexpected for the non-working weeks of the year.

Over a decade ago, the Myer Inquiry looked into the possibility of providing enhanced stipends and taxation benefits for visual artists.[49] The inquiry asked whether Australia should follow the path taken in other countries including Canada, Ireland and the Netherlands. With considerable popular support, those governments formed the view that the status of the artist was and is a matter of national pride which should be backed up by favourable economic and taxation treatment. Some of these have been pulled back since the Global Financial Crisis; and a number of the former Eastern Bloc countries no longer single out artistic practitioners for state-sponsored benefit. Yet many European countries still maintain the status of the artist legislation, unemployment benefits for the self-employed, tax exemptions and subsidised pensions.[50] The Myer Inquiry concluded that forms of state-sanctioned respect for the artist would not sit well with government or the Australian public.

There were precedents much closer to home: as early as 1909 Prime Minister Alfred Deacon set up the Commonwealth Literary Fund to support writers; but, with the setting up of the Australia Council, the ex gratia payments gradually dwindled in favour of a more bureaucratised and hence democratically transparent process. Outside the status conferred by the Australian honours system (which does not itself pay any bills or confer any financial benefits) the country remains egalitarian in the sense that beyond the very small prize-culture of Prime Minister's and Premier's Awards, those who reach the pinnacles of art or science are not singled out for any form of public financial reward. At the risk of beating a tired old drum, the same cannot be said for sport.

The tax system also presents problems for workers in the performing arts whose norm is to be employed but only for short periods or with multiple employers. They also work other jobs or have separate careers and use these to cross-subsidise their income. Adverse superannuation impacts are discussed in the next section. A more complex problem, which creates daily difficulties for artists, agents, companies and administrators, is the interaction of the Australian system for PAYG taxation, superannuation, workers' compensation and intellectual property ownership, of which each has a different test to tell whether or not an individual is employed.

The trite solution is for every individual in the

performing arts to run themselves as a business through a Pty Ltd company. In reality, this becomes conceivable at income levels of $40,000 per year and just about viable when contractor income levels reach around $70,000—though company structures are designed for businesses turning over many more times than that. The compliance burden, including GST and separate tax accounting, insurance and banking fees, is rarely appealing to those who live from job to job with periods of inactivity in between.

At the other end of the scale is the debate between the tax authorities and artists as to whether their activities would be better treated as a hobby. The decision in *Pedley* was mentioned Chapter 1. It was something of a test case not only for the artist but the status of the artist, and reinforced the Taxation Commissioner's surprisingly enlightened statement that:

> *The fact that a taxpayer's motives are idealistic rather than mercenary will not prevent a conclusion that the taxpayer is engaged in carrying on a business.*[51]

The fact remains that many artists do not have the financial resources to get with the business tax system and it will prejudice access to the social security system. This is where status of the artist legislation has potential to do some good.

In Australia we got where we are by dismantling old systems of self-help on the promise of the welfare state.

We have now dismantled significant parts of the welfare state that weren't working well politically; and we have bolted on a series of small legislated schemes such as performers' rights in copyright, small concessions in the industrial awards, income averaging and relaxation of the 'hobbyist' rules. At the same time, technology and other manifestations of the cost disease have squeezed creators and artists' incomes and working conditions. Where do we go from here?

## The Superannuation Funds and the Superannuation Guarantee Charge (SGC)

Once again, the asymmetry between employer self-help and relatively small efforts to support the freelance or short-term performer has increased, not decreased, in the twenty years since the Fair Work Act altered the ninety-year-old Australian industrial relations system beyond recognition. Yes, WorkCover and its equivalents, unemployment and disability benefits, are theoretically available to performers and crews, but the reality is that they do not, and by their structure cannot, support practitioners in what is all too often a profession in which underemployment is a chronic condition. Media Super, the principal industry superannuation fund, which covers both performers and media personnel, conducted an online survey in April-May 2015 of members and received 2,550 responses. To quote the executive summary:

> *...the majority of entertainment and arts professionals believe that the sector is hugely important to Australian culture; however, only 17 per cent say that the Australian Government respects and values the arts. Shockingly, only 9 per cent rate the government's performance in investing and supporting the arts as good, while 64 per cent believe it's poor. Sadly 64 per cent of those working in entertainment and arts are also regularly giving work away for free in the hope of furthering their career or securing a paying job, and 59 per cent are concerned they might lose their job or main source of income in the next twelve months.*[52]

Sixty-two per cent of members in the entertainment and arts sector considered they would not have enough superannuation to live a comfortable retirement; ahead of 49 and 46 per cent in journalism and the print industry respectively.

Working from the latest annual returns published by the Australian Prudential Regulation Authority, (APRA), Media Super's membership statistics are similar to a number of other funds.[53] Out of 78,472 members and just over $3 billion in its funds, the number of members tails off dramatically in the over 50s age groupings. APRA has urged caution on these figures as it is a relatively new series but, as a proportion of all age groups, the 45 to 84 demographic comprises just 16 per cent of the whole membership. Again, rough numbers indicate that the average amount of super held in the account of any member aged between 45 and 84 is $58,000. Australian crews have historically been contributors to the much larger Australian Super. Even though backstage staff are more likely to be employed and for longer, it has not been possible to isolate a figure for crews from the Australian Super returns.

This state of affairs has occurred despite the benefit of a very specific provision in the superannuation legislation which mandates everyone working in the entertainment industry, irrespective of whether they are treated as independent contractors, must receive superannuation contributions from anyone who pays them.[54] This is also true for crews and technicians in film, TV and other recorded entertainment.

By contrast, the figure for university academics in the tertiary education sector's fund, Unisuper, shows an average for the over-45 age group of nearly three times that of Media Super at $144,000 per head. The university sector, like the performing arts sector, includes people in support and infrastructure roles, not just creative and innovative ones. Long-term employment in the university sector has been replaced by serial short-term appointments at the post-doctoral level—but 'short-term' still means six-month to three-year contracts, dependent on funding. In the performing arts, short-term, often very short-term, employment is the norm, but the university sector is also committed to building member savings. Many universities include an element of salary sacrifice to super plus additional contributions above the compulsory 9.5 per cent figure.

What is also different is that many contracts from individual producers or venues will fall below the $450/month figure where SGC must be paid, even though the individual may be earning more than that by working for different employers through each month. All performers are likely to be able to boost superannuation savings through access to a low-income superannuation contribution, fixed at a maximum of $500 per year with eligibility capped at incomes below $37,000. After 1 July 2017, this took the form of a rebate on tax paid.[55] It might sound beneficial if government is going to keep this up for the next forty years but the scheme only started in 2012, is not indexed and is next to meaningless for someone over 45, let alone 55.

There are many things about these figures which will only firm up as the data is gathered over time, but what is clear now is that of the Media Super members, which include journalists and other workers in media, the *maximum* average amount an actor in middle age to old age currently has in their superannuation account is $58,000. Performers are certainly far more likely to be contributing to the bottom end of that average across all Media Super members. To say that performers and other members of the performing arts sector do not see themselves as having a 'comfortable' old age is a massive understatement.

Compulsory universal superannuation came into force in 1992. Both the Media Super findings, and any discussion among performers particularly, confirm that after

25 years the compulsory levy cannot provide adequate retirement support for professionals who have not had continuous paid employment. This is one area where the superannuation funds differ from the benevolent and mutual funds of old. The benevolent funds in particular had the character of collectively organised, mutually supportive emergency funds, with discretion to advance moneys to anyone in need whether in or out of employment and irrespective of any one individual's contribution during a time of prosperity. Even then, these schemes were attempts to paper over a gap that was structural. The current structure allows people in the performing arts to fall right through. Indeed, the gaps have become wider since the scheme was first introduced.

Critical to the duties of contemporary regulated superannuation funds is the 'sole purpose test' which is further split into 'core purposes', which require (on pain of civil penalties) that no moneys may be advanced to anyone other than a member prior to retirement; and 'ancillary purposes' which permit provision of benefits to the member where cessation of work is on account of ill health (physical or mental); or to the member's estate after their death.[56]

Until 1 July 1997, the funds had discretion to advance money to members of the relevant industries who were experiencing 'hardship or misfortune'. The rationale for phasing out that option was that superannuation had to be accumulated for retirement purposes and not advanced earlier on any but the most stringent grounds.[57] Benefits may be paid out in circumstances of temporary incapacity (where paid sick leave is not available) or on compassionate grounds.[58] What is not possible are the sorts of micro-payments, let alone micro-loans that have driven successful social credit systems around the world. In terms of supporting members through expensive crises, no funds may be advanced to anyone beyond the amount standing to their account in the fund. One of the very principles of the collective in both socialism and most of the world's religions 'from each according to their ability, to each according to their needs' is abrogated in favour of the individual ledger.

APRA has indicated that trustees of the funds are entitled to provide benefits outside the core and ancillary purposes from their own profits (inapplicable in the case of industry funds) or may conduct investment activities that may indirectly benefit members.[59] Media Super, for example, has invested over $150 million in Australian television production. At the risk of my sounding naïf, low cost social benefit housing is equally an investment with which the core purpose test could readily be met; but the reality is, at present, that superannuation funds in the Australian system are severely restricted, even among industry funds which, after all, are the biggest beneficiaries of the accumulated savings of those in the industry.

No one is being wilful here. These are the rules based on the policy settings arrived at by government over 25 years ago to help individuals fund their retirement, not their working lives; but if one looks at whole of life issues for performers, the lack of support for individuals during their career, for all but the most dire circumstances, means there is yet another gap in the social network that might otherwise support individuals faced with the sort of problems people have in the performing arts.

# 6. From problems to solutions

From my own observation of the Australian and, to a lesser extent, English performing arts scene, anyone of my generation who expected to have a career in the performing arts needed to start with the price of a house. That's right, *start* with it. But that has huge implications.

Was it the same in previous generations? Possibly. One can certainly think of the Australian stars like Helen Mitchell/Nellie Melba who came from prosperous middle-class backgrounds; but, jumping forward, there were other paths, particularly for the immediate post-World War Two generation, who maintained their training and relationship with their teachers, unlike their European counterparts so severely disrupted by the conflict. To me, the generation of Australians who in the 1950s and early 60s descended on Covent Garden, Sadlers Wells and, to a lesser extent, the BBC, Broadway and British and US film, often came from humble families in the Australian suburbs. Such families as asked their teachers whether their child could earn a living as a dancer or a singer. For, if not, they would get a job in a bank or a shop.[60] Of course they also won scholarships or competitions (such as competitions like the Australian *Women's Weekly* in dance, the *Sun* Aria competition, or the Mobil Quest, which discovered Joan Sutherland) funded by a public who believed that to launch a talented child across the ocean was enough.

## It's also about place

A house itself is a burden; but the price of a house? This is the same issue, curiously, as for a fledgling performing arts company that yearns for a home, but finds that the cost of maintaining it in the end proves the death of the enterprise. So much better to have the *price* of a home—and even more so for the specialist performer who, because of the relentless need to find new audiences, must never settle but wander the globe in search of yet another success. In proposing a collective response to the structural problems of performers' welfare, housing is central and the times are such that it is now glaringly obvious. Wasn't this sorted out a century ago?

In a way, yes. In fact, not only have we done it before but Australia did it early. Surprisingly, many people still think today that a dedicated institution exists in Victoria for the support of elderly members of the theatrical profession. Known then and now as The Old Colonists' Association of Victoria (OCAV), it was founded in 1869 by a group of passionate believers in self-help, including George Coppin, the largest figure on the Australian stage at the time. This was followed shortly by the Australasian

Dramatic and Musical Association in 1871, predating the UK Actors' Benevolent Fund by ten years. Coppin was a theatrical entrepreneur, politician, property developer and Freemason who made three fortunes and lost two. He also helped make the fortunes of English actors Charles and Ellen Kean on tour in the 1860s and who afterwards took part in setting up the UK Benevolent Fund. Not only did Coppin and other committee members secure four and a half acres beside Merri Creek for the association but another four and a half for the welfare of actors and related disciplines, which merged together in 1907. Today the OCAV is a very substantial charitable provider of care with four facilities throughout Victoria.[61] Even after the merger, the Rushall Park complex, as it is also known, was portrayed in picture postcards of the time as 'The Dramatic Homes'.[62]

## And what about overseas?

In the UK, the Actors' Benevolent Fund, also mentioned before, sits alongside the Actors' Charitable Trust and the Actors' Homes, known generally after actor-manager and English MP Alfred Denville as Denville Hall.[63] In addition to the Royal Variety Performance, the Royal Variety Charity Fund started receiving money from the phone voting in the US for *Britain's Got Talent* in 2007. It supports the 36-room Brinsworth House in Twickenham, opened in 1911.[64] Co-incidentally, it was Melbourne-born Sir Oswald Stoll who created the Stoll-Moss chain of Empire and Colosseum Theatres throughout Britain who supported the British funds between the wars as the Australian equivalents dwindled. He also created a separate foundation, still in existence, to provide homes for ex-service men and women.[65] For dance and opera there is the Royal Opera House Benevolent Fund for past employees and dependents of the Covent Garden and Royal Birmingham companies.[66] Like the Australian funds, they draw on grass roots knowledge of those who may need help, and, (unlike the Australian funds) offer housing as one of the available strategies.

Across the Atlantic, the first Actors' Fund home was dedicated in New York in 1902 as wider acceptance of the profession grew from the Actors' Fund's purchase of a burial ground. It now supports extensive rent-controlled and dedicated housing throughout the country. It has also developed health initiatives, and specialised clinics and programs on career transition for dancers.[67]

One final example. In Milan Giuseppe Verdi founded the Casa di Riposo per Musicisti, popularly known as the Casa Verdi, for opera singers and musicians in reduced circumstances. Verdi and his wife, Giuseppina Strepponi, designed the building with the architect Camillo Boito, paid for construction and it was opened in 1899 after his death. The Verdis are buried there and the royalties from Verdi's operas, among other benefactions from opera greats, help fund its operations. It has also recently provided accommodation for younger artists, some of whom receive stipends for providing part-time care for their elders.

In a letter to his friend Giulio Monteverde, Verdi, wrote:

> *Of all my works, my favourite is the home that I had built in Milan to care for elderly artists who did not possess the virtue of putting some savings aside in their youth. My poor and dear life's companions! Please believe me, my friend, when I say that this Home is my masterpiece.*[68]

The old ways might never have been the best ways and they are largely vestigial in Australia. Among conditions that are all too common for a country like ours, of poverty and social isolation, a home of one's own, among one's own, needs revisiting.

# 7. Conclusion

So, what practical steps could be taken to fix the problems with which we find ourselves today?

- The industry superannuation funds might look at the provisions of their trust deeds and set up and administer emergency and other charitable support for members of the industries they cover; not limited to the individual balances of members of the fund but out of specific reserves which would not infringe the ancillary purpose test of the SGIC.
- The commercial funds likewise should have elements of social responsibility further built in to support their members and the wider community.
- Government, in addition to low-balance support for superannuation, might consider a further supplement based on the salary sacrifice principles common in other sectors (and this includes the relatively low-paid university sector) under which individuals in relatively good times of well-paid work could make additional contributions to their super via the PAYG system.

- Another supplement (not a new suggestion) would be a levy of as little as five cents on every ticket to live performance sold in Australia to support a similar fund.
- An immediate need is a greater concentration, in training and within companies and the theatrical community, and funding for dealing with health and mental health issues in the performing arts.
- Performing arts education institutions, including those run privately, must not be afraid to talk about the downside of being a creative performer, the protocols of good performance and the economics of the industry. Aspirants should graduate with a realistic understanding of the choices available and the networks to support them; that talent on its own is not enough: that performance is a competitive business and success does not come just by 'wanting it enough'.
- Industry unions and producers, together with the major state-funded performing arts companies, must look above the hard graft of day-to-day issues and strengthen recent initiatives to encourage whole-of-life support even in a business with high short-term commercial risks, rocky long-term financing prospects and a reliance on youth, mobility and internationalism.
- The work of the actors' benevolent funds and

> related institutions must be inclusive, be clear on unified messages, speak to the discrepant and fragmented nature of the sector and avoid divisions of employment between 'legitimate' theatre, the media, variety and cabaret, circus, backstage and front-of-house.

Finally, and, in my view, based on all of the above, housing and access to emergency accommodation has to be available both for working individuals and those in permanent or semi-retirement at or near to the major capital cities. For this there are the models which existed under the former rules of the Old Colonists' Association in Victoria (sometimes actually known as the 'Dramatic Homes') and with ample precedent at Denville Hall in London and the Actors' Fund homes in the United States. Investment in social housing and social capital schemes through superannuation funds or industry forms are a vital part of the mix. And let us not forget the philanthropy of individuals who have been kind to art or show business through long-term contributions with far-reaching effects. Too many professional participants in the Australian performing arts are falling through gaps that were supposed to be solved by labour market reforms and compulsory superannuation. Regrettably, the way to fix these deficiencies is to go back and create an alternative future.

When next we're in that actor's bar at the end of a show, we need to be sure that breaking out the booze and having a ball is not all there is.

# Appendix

## Working in the Australian entertainment industry: A research project by Entertainment Assist in association with College of Arts, Victoria University, October 2016. Extract from key findings*

### WHO PARTICIPATED:

- 2904 respondents across all sectors of the entertainment industry from all States and Territories of Australia.

**Group 1: Performing artists and music composers** (including musicians, radio presenters, actors, singers, entertainers or variety artists, dancers or choreographers, television presenters, composers, music professionals and music directors)
**Group 2: Performing arts support workers** (including media producers, film and video editors, program directors, directors, production assistants, video producers, film, television and stage directors, technical directors, make-up artists, directors of photography, stage managers, venue managers and artistic directors)
**Group 3: Broadcasting, film and recorded media equipment operators** (includes sound technicians, camera operators, projectionists, light technicians, television equipment operators, roadies and performing arts technicians)

## WORK AND SLEEP PATTERNS:

Working unpredictable hours

- 43.1% of entertainment industry workers work most of the time in the evenings and night.
- 41.9% work on the weekends.
- 30.2% always work unpredictable hours.

This is well over general population shift work patterns where 16% of the general population are shift workers.

Sleep disorders

- 44% of entertainment industry workers don't get enough sleep.
- 45.5% have disrupted sleep.
- 6% of the Australian population has a chronic sleep disorder. Thus, entertainment industry workers suffer sleep disorders seven times greater than the general population.

Insomnia

- 16% of entertainment industry workers suffer from insomnia which is three times greater than general population at 5.6%.

| Group 1: PERFORMERS who most of the time/always: | Actors | Dancers | Musicians | Singers | Other performing artists |
|---|---|---|---|---|---|
| Work in the evenings and night | 43.3% | 65.5% | 57.3% | 61.2% | 38.3% |
| Work on the weekends | 51.6% | 75.2% | 66.9% | 61.2% | 73.6% |
| Work unpredictable hours | 55.3% | 49.6% | 60.6% | 38.8% | 58.8% |
| Don't get enough sleep | 64.6% | 75.2% | 65.1% | 53.8% | 47% |
| Have disrupted sleep | 60.9% | 68.2% | 64.7% | 74.7% | 53% |
| Suffer insomnia | 39.5% | 51.7% | 46.3% | 41.8% | 38.2% |

| Group 2: SUPPORT WORKERS who most of the time/always: | Stage managers | Technical directors | Other perf arts support workers |
|---|---|---|---|
| Work in the evenings and night | 72.9% | 59.6% | 35.4% |
| Work on the weekends | 74.6% | 63.8% | 36.2% |
| Work unpredictable hours | 72.9% | 68.1% | 48% |
| Don't get enough sleep | 74.6% | 74.5% | 73.3% |
| Have disrupted sleep | 78% | 78.7% | 69.3% |
| Suffer insomnia | 50.9% | 55.3% | 47.3% |

| Group 3: TECHS/ CREW/ROADIES who most of the time/always: | Lighting technicians | Sound technicians | Road crew and riggers |
|---|---|---|---|
| Work in the evenings and night | 76.1% | 78.5% | 78.7% |
| Work on the weekends | 77% | 81.8% | 78.8% |
| Work unpredictable hours | 77.1% | 76% | 78.8% |
| Don't get enough sleep | 85.4% | 76.8% | 75.7% |
| Have disrupted sleep | 60.6% | 74.4% | 84.4% |
| Suffer insomnia | 43.1% | 53.7% | 57.6% |

## Impact of irregular work patterns and sleep disorders

- 57.9% of entertainment industry workers have problems finding time for their families.
- 63% have trouble maintaining a social life.
- 45% have trouble keeping contact with their friends in the industry.

## MENTAL HEALTH:

Diagnosis of a mental health disorder in their lifetime

- The most common mental health diagnoses reported across the three groups is depression followed by anxiety.
- 44% of industry workers have moderate to severe anxiety. This is 10 times higher than the general population.
- The levels of depression symptoms are five times higher than general population scores.

| | Group 1 | Group 2 | Group 3 |
|---|---|---|---|
| Diagnosed with a mental illness | 40.8% | 37.5% | 31% |
| Diagnosis of more than one mental illness over a lifetime | 34.6% | 37.3% | 39.8% |

| Group 1: PERFORMERS: | Actors | Dancers | Musicians | Singers | Variety artists |
|---|---|---|---|---|---|
| Diagnosed with mental illness | 21.4% | 12.9% | 23.4% | 21.4% | 27.9% |
| Moderate to severe depression | 53.5% | 29.2% | 54.1% | 54.1% | 67.4% |
| Moderate to severe anxiety | 25.6% | 25.3% | 24.4% | 19.4% | 34.9% |

| Group 2: SUPPORT WORKERS | Stage managers | Technical directors | Other perf arts support workers |
|---|---|---|---|
| Diagnosed with mental illness | 17.4% | 13.6% | 28.5% |
| Moderate to severe depression | 60.5% | 67.8% | 58.1% |
| Moderate to severe anxiety | 26.7% | 32.2% | 25.1% |

| Group 3: TECHS/CREW/ ROADIES | Lighting technicians | Sound technicians | Road crew and riggers |
|---|---|---|---|
| Diagnosed with mental illness | 20.1% | 20.2% | 24.4% |
| Moderate to severe depression | 64.6% | 63.8% | 64.4% |
| Moderate to severe anxiety | 39.6% | 30.1% | 31.3% |

Sought professional assistance for mental health issues

- Overall 59.5% of entertainment industry workers have sought professional assistance for their mental health issues.

| | Group 1 | Group 2 | Group 3 |
|---|---|---|---|
| Sought professional assistance | 65.2% | 59.6% | 45.2% |

## SOCIAL SUPPORT AND NETWORKS:

- 59.9% of industry workers could not raise $2000 from their networks in an emergency.
- 56.1% feel they either cannot get help or only sometimes receive help from friends, family, neighbours and colleagues when in need.

Most entertainment industry workers do not know where to get support from in the entertainment industry and identify critical barriers to seeking support including:

1. lack of resources such as time, money and lack of good support resources;
2. problems inherent in the industry such as lack of trust, unsupportive environment, disjointed lifestyle, lack of respect for industry from outside;
3. a perception that seeking support may compromise future employment opportunities.

| Group 1: PERFORMERS: | Actors | Dancers | Musicians | Singers | Variety artists |
|---|---|---|---|---|---|
| Cannot raise $2K in an emergency | 60% | 79.1% | 60.5% | 51.7% | 46.7% |
| Feel they cannot garner support from friends, family or colleagues | 49.4% | 57.1% | 49% | 47.5% | 56.6% |
| Do not know where to find support within the industry | 48% | 46.2% | 51.4% | 50.7% | 38.2% |

| Group 2: SUPPORT WORKERS | Stage managers | Technical directors | Other perf arts support workers |
|---|---|---|---|
| Cannot raise $2K in an emergency | 55.2% | 54.6% | 47.5% |
| Feel they cannot garner support from friends, family or colleagues | 51.7% | 63.6% | 58.4% |
| Do not know where to find support within the industry | 57.7% | 48.9% | 52.7% |

| Group 3: TECHS/CREW/ ROADIES | Lighting technicians | Sound technicians | Road crew and riggers |
|---|---|---|---|
| Cannot raise $2K in an emergency | 56% | 69.3% | 81.8% |
| Feel they cannot garner support from friends, family or colleagues | 63.3% | 65.2% | 72.7% |
| Do not know where to find support within the industry | 52.3% | 62.8% | 54.5% |

## SUICIDE:

Suicide ideation and planning

- Suicide attempts for Australian entertainment industry workers are more than double that of the general population.

- In the last twelve months road crew members experienced suicide ideation almost nine times more than general population.
- In the last twelve months Australian Entertainment Industry Workers experience suicide ideation from five to seven times more than the general population and two to three times more over a lifetime.
- Suicide planning for Australian Entertainment Industry workers is four to five times more than general population.

Suicide ideation responses: Group

| | Performers | Support Workers | Tech / crew / roadies | All groups | General Population (Johnston et al, 2009) | Entertainment Industry Rate compared to General Population |
|---|---|---|---|---|---|---|
| Suicide ideation in the last 12 months | 13.1% | 15.6% | 19.1% | 14.8% | 2.3% | 6 times greater |
| Suicide ideation in their lifetime | 26.4% | 31% | 33.6% | 28.9% | 13.3% | More than double |
| Suicide planning | 16% | 17.5% | 19.9% | 17.4% | 4% | 4-5 times greater |
| Suicide attempts | 7.4% | 7.9% | 8.5% | 7.7% | 3.2% | More than double |

## Suicide ideation responses: Performers

| | Actors | Dancers | Musicians | Singers | General population (Johnston et al, 2009) |
|---|---|---|---|---|---|
| Suicide Ideation in the last 12 months | 14.9% | 7.1% | 15.3% | 12.2% | 2.3% |
| Suicide Ideation in their Lifetime | 30.2% | 15.7% | 30% | 22.4% | 13.3% |
| Suicide Planning | 18.1% | 8.6% | 18.4% | 16.6% | 4% |
| Suicide Attempts | 8% | 3.7% | 7.5% | 10.2% | 3.2% |

## Suicidal ideation responses: Technical and support

| | Road crew | Lighting techs | Sound techs | 'Other' support workers | General population (Johnston et al, 2009) |
|---|---|---|---|---|---|
| Suicide ideation in the last 12 months | 20% | 18.8% | 19% | 16.8% | 2.3% |
| Suicide ideation in their lifetime | 35.6% | 29.9% | 33.7% | 33% | 13.3% |
| Suicide planning | 17.8% | 21.5% | 17.8% | 20.7% | 4% |
| Suicide attempts | 4.4% | 7.6% | 8.6% | 10.1% | 3.2% |

* The permission of Entertainment Assist to reproduce these tables is gratefully acknowledged.

# Endnotes

All the digital references accessed by the author are still valid at the time of publication.

1 Michael Hutter and David Throsby (eds): *Beyond Price. Value in Culture, Economics and the Arts* (Cambridge: Cambridge University Press) 2008.

2 *Pedley v. FC of T* [2006] AATA 108; 2006 ATC 2064; (2006) 62 ATR 1014 which concluded that a professional art business *was* being carried on.

3 Blair Edgar OAM, personal communication.

4 https://actorsfund.org/about-us/history

5 https://www.actorsbenevolentfund.co.uk/about/history#2000s

6 STC, MTC and QTC annual reports for 2017; cinema figures calculated from www.screenaustralia.gov.au/fact-finders/cinema/industry-trends/box-office/australian-box-office; and Rebecca Mostyn, 'Explainer: Where's the Audience for Australian Films?' 17 January 2014, theconversation.com

7 Jeanette Liddell, personal communication, January 2018.

8 Blair Edgar OAM, personal communication, January 2018.

9 David Throsby and Katya Petatskaya, *Making Art Work: An Economic Study of Professional Artists in Australia* (Sydney: Australia Council) 2017.

www.australiacouncil.gov.au/workspace/uploads/files/making-art-work-throsby-report-5a05106d0bb69.pdf (Fig 9.1 p.87). Table 8.8 (p. 85) suggests actors' and directors' incomes have halved to an average of $9,000 per annum.

10 Jackson Browne, 'Before the Deluge' in *Late for the Sky* (1974).

11 David Throsby and Anita Zednik, *Do You Really Expect to Get Paid? An Economic Study of Professional Artists in Australia* (Sydney: Australia Council) 2010. http://www.australiacouncil.gov.au/workspace/uploads/files/do_you_really_expect_to_get_pa-591bc90705ff8.pdf

12 The comparison is between the categories in Fig. 9.1, p.87 of the 2017 study and Fig. 17 on p 53 of the 2010 publication.

13 Throsby and Petatskaya Appendix II Table 9.4 p.228.

14 Throsby and Zednik Appendix II Table 36 p.127.

15 *Making Art Work.* I am extremely grateful to Dr Petatskaya for guiding me to the right sections of these reports and identifying points of difference between the two studies.

16 Brent Salter and M.R. Williams, 'Performers and the Digital Environment—the 'Australian Experience'. Paper presented at the Australian National University Centre for International and Public Law Conference Copyright 2010: 'A Decade of Moral Rights and the Digital Agenda', 21–22 June 2010.

17 Kimberley Weatherall, 'Pretend-y Rights: On the Insanely Complicated New Regime in Australia, and How Australian Performers Lost Out'; in Fiona Macmillan and Kathy Bowrey, *New Directions in*

*Copyright Law* Vol. 3 (Cheltenham UK: Edward Elgar) 2006, pp.171–97, p.187.

18 Julie van den Eynde, Adrian Fisher, Christopher Sonn, *Pride, Passion and Pitfalls: Working in the Australian Entertainment Industry* (Maribyrnong, Melbourne: Entertainment Assist, Victoria University), December 2014 pp.1-2 quoting the *West Australian*, 2013, http://au.news.yahoo.com/thewest/entertainment/a/-/music/15803423/roadies-life-not-so-rocknroll/

19 See, for example, Sanna M. Nordin Bates, Jennifer Cumming, Diana Always, Lucinda Sharp, 'Imagining Yourself Dancing to Perfection? Correlates of Perfectionism Among Ballet and Contemporary Dancers', *Journal of Clinical Sport Psychology*, 2011, 5, 58-76.

20 Tony Watts and Genevieve Picot, *John Hargreaves…a celebration* (Parrot: npp, Australia, 2000), pp.268-69. Quoted by permission of the authors.

21 *Making Art Work*, Appendix II Table 3.3 p.187; general comparison with the labour force Figure 3.5 p.31.

22 *Making Art Work*, Figure 3.3 p.29.

23 *Making Art Work*, Chapter 12 pp.123–34.

24 *Making Art Work*, Table 12.1 p. 124. See also Lindy Hume, *Restless Giant: Changing cultural values in Regional Australia*. Platform Paper No.50, 2017.

25 James Waites, *Whatever Happened to the STC Actors' Company?* Platform Paper No.23, April 2010, pp. 31, 45.

26 The Throsby-Petatskaya study used NESB as its category to maintain uniformity with the previous data sets but

points out Cultural and Linguistic Diversity (CALD) is the favoured measurement, p.143. The study therefore does not distinguish between English-speakers with Indigenous and non-Indigenous backgrounds.

27 Throsby-Petatskaya, p.30, Figure 3.4; and Table 3.2 Appendix II p.186.

28 Julie van den Eynde, Professor Adrian Fisher, Christopher Sonn, *Working in the Australian Entertainment Industry*: Final Report (Maribyrnong, Melbourne: Entertainment Assist, Victoria University), October 2016, pp.22–25.

29 Green Room Awards Association, Annual Awards programmes 2003-13, in possession of the author.

30 David Throsby, 'Economic Circumstances of the Performing Artist: Baumol and Bowen Thirty Years On' *Journal of Cultural Economics*, vol. 20, 1996, 225-240

31 Alex Bagot, *Coppin The Great, Father of the Australian Theatre* (Melbourne: Melbourne University Press), 1965, p.14 et passim.

32 Actors' Benevolent Fund (UK): https://www.actorsbenevolentfund.co.uk/

33 *The Lorgnette*, Thursday 2 August 1894, p.3. The Australasian Dramatic and Musical Association was formed in November 1871. It met with initial indifference from other colonies and active rebuff from Victoria's Governor, Sir John Manners Sutton, Viscount Canterbury, who suggested they merge with the Society for the Relief of the Educated Poor: *Weekly Times*, 27 January 1872, pp.10-11. It lost its cash in the bank 'smash'

of 1892: *Argus*, 15 February 1894, p.6. The land it held for housing indigent actors was transferred to the Old Colonists' Association by Act of Parliament in 1907. After nearly seventy years, its final assets also appear to have been transferred to the Old Colonists' Association in June 1940: *Argus*, 17 June 1940, p.6. However a report in the *Sydney Sportsman*, 17 June 1914, p.3, stated that the assets had been transferred at that stage to the Actors' Association of Australasia, Sydney.

34 *Illustrated Australasian News*, 1 August 1894, pp.4-6; *The Lorgnette*, Thursday 2 August 1894, p 2. Held on 18 July 1894 at the Melbourne Cricket Ground between two teams of male characters and female characters (all played by men). It was followed by a Ladies' Harlequin Bicycle Race and raised £1,000 to replenish funds lost in the bank crash: *Lorgnette*, 5 July 1894, *Argus*, 7 July 1894. A sole programme for a Distressed Actors' Fund benefit at the Princess Theatre on 16 December 1899 is held in the Yarra Valley Library, Victoria, though many newspaper reports record regular benefit concerts from the 1870s and fundraising measures by George Coppin, regarded by some as extortion: St Kilda, Prahran and South Yarra *Guardian and Telegraph*, 6 November 1875.

35 Frank van Straten has been kind enough to provide me with copies of the Rules and Annual returns of J.C. Williamson's Comic Opera Company Fund for 1906 and the Tivoli Circuit Staff Superannuation Plan: Frank van Straten AM, personal archive.

36 Derek Latham, personal communication, January 2018.

37 http://liveperformance.com.au/industry_service_fee_isf

38 https://www.fairwork.gov.au/ending-employment/bankruptcy-and-liquidation

39 Personal communications.

40 The 'cost disease' in the arts is a whole topic in itself. Put simply, increased productivity has its limits: you cannot perform a string quartet with two players doing the work of four, though that is pretty much what we see today down in the pit of big stage musicals where the musical director is also playing multiple keyboards. A select bibliography might include William J Baumol, and Harold Bowen, *The Performing Arts: The Economic Dilemma* (New York: Twentieth Century Fund) 1966; David Throsby and Glenn Withers, *The Economics of the Performing Arts* (London: Edward Arnold) 1979; Ruth Towse, *Baumol's Cost Disease, The Arts and Other Victims* (Cheltenham: Edward Elgar) 1997.

41 The then Federal Shadow Arts Minister, Peter Garrett, announced a proposal, ArtStart, to harmonise criteria for artists across government and address perennial financial sustainability problems. http://www.chass.org.au/media-releases/labor-announces-its-vision-for-the-arts/

It was Labor's New Directions for the Arts policy associated with the successful 2007 election campaign. Once in government it morphed into a grant scheme analogous to the New Enterprise Initiative Scheme (NEIS).

42 http://www.actorsbenevolentfund.org.au/

43 Letter from Mr C.L. McVilly, Victorian Inspector of Charities, to Mr Hal Alexander, Actors Equity

Foundation, 8 November 1944 (VABT Archives 1944 C-04).

44 http://abfqld.com.au

45 https://supportact.org.au/

46 https://www.entertainmentassist.org.au/about-us/

47 https://www.humanservices.gov.au/individuals/services/centrelink/newstart-allowance

48 Division 405 of the Income Tax Assessment Act 1997 (formerly Division 16A ITAA 1936) provides for income averaging for significant fluctuations in the income of Australian resident writers, artists, inventors, sportspersons, composers, performers and production associates.

49 Parliament of Australia, Report of the Contemporary Visual Arts and Craft Inquiry (Canberra: Dept. of Communications, Information Technology and the Arts, 2002) 'The Myer Inquiry'. http://www.dcita.gov.au/__data/assets/pdf_file/12087/Report_of_the_Contemporary_Visual_Arts_and_Craft_Inquiry.pdf

50 Compendium: Cultural Policies and Trends in Europe https://www.culturalpolicies.net/web/comparisons-tables.php?aid=34andcid=45andlid=en. My thanks to Matthew Emond for referring me to this site.

51 Australian Taxation Office, Taxation Ruling TR2005/01—Carrying on business as a Professional Artist par 20A.

52 https://www.mediasuper.com.au/about-our-community/industry-trends

53 http://www.apra.gov.au/Super/Publications/Pages/Annual-MySuper-Statistics.aspx

54 Section 12(8) of the *Superannuation Guarantee (Administration) Act 1992* (SGAA). It was contained in the original 1992 legislation but the Explanatory Memorandum does not explain why the Government chose specifically to mandate SGC for participants in entertainment and sport.

55 https://www.ato.gov.au/Rates/key-superannuation-rates-and-thresholds/?anchor=Lowincomesuperannuationcontribution#Lowincomesuperannuationcontribution

56 *Superannuation Industry (Supervision) Act 1993* (Cth) s.62.

57 APRA, Superannuation Circular No III.A.4 pars 25 and 26 (February 2001): http://www.apra.gov.au/super/documents/iii-a-4-the-sole-purpose-test.pdf

58 Regs 5.08, 6.01(2), 6.19A and Schedule 1(Part 1); APRA Superannuation Circular I.C.2 September 2006 pars 84-88, 98-100: http://www.apra.gov.au/Super/Documents/Superannuation-Circular-I-C-2-Payments-Standards-for-Regulated-Superannuation-Funds.pdf

59 APRA Circular III.A.4 pars 34-42.

60 Patricia Laughlin, *Marilyn Jones 'A Brilliance All Her Own* (Melbourne: Quartet, 1978) pp.16–18; Lauris Elms, *The Singing Elms: the autobiography of Lauris Elms* (Bowerbird Press: Terrey Hills, NSW, 2001); June Bronhill, *The Merry Bronhill: an autobiography* (Mandarin, Port Melbourne, 1990); Anna Bemrose *Robert Helpmann: a Servant of Art* (St Lucia: University of Queensland Press, 2008).

61 https://ocav.com.au/app/uloads/2015/11/Rushall_Old_Colonists.pdf
62 State Library of Victoria Picture Collection a03441.
63 https://www.denvillehall.org.uk/about
64 http://www.royalvarietycharity.org/brinsworth-house
65 Stoll Mansions, next to Chelsea Football Ground, contains accommodation for 157 residents https://www.stoll.org.uk/about/history/; https://en.wikipedia.org/wiki/Oswald_Stoll
66 www.roh.org.uk/about/benevolent fund
67 www.actorsfund.org/about-us/history
68 https://www.casaverdi.it/en/; https://en.wikipedia.org/wiki/Casa_di_Riposo_per_Musicisti

# COPYRIGHT INFORMATION

PLATFORM PAPERS
Quarterly essays from Currency House Inc.
Founding Editor: Dr John Golder
Editor: Katharine Brisbane
Currency House Inc. is a non-profit association and resource centre advocating the role of the performing arts in public life by research, debate and publication.

Postal address: PO Box 2270, Strawberry Hills, NSW 2012, Australia
Email: info@currencyhouse.org.au Tel: (02) 9319 4953
Website: www.currencyhouse.org.au Fax: (02) 9319 3649



ISBN 978-0-9946130-9-7
ISSN 1449-583X

Typeset in Garamond
Printed by Ligare Book Printers, Riverwood, NSW
Production by Currency Press Pty Ltd

# FORTHCOMING

## PP No.57, November 2018

## CULTURAL RIGHTS:
### A contemporary issue
### Scott Rankin

What are cultural rights and why are they in crisis? Put simply in the author's words: 'Everyone, everywhere has a right to thrive.' Society is made of insiders and outsiders, victors and vanquished, land holders and asylum seekers; and while in Australia we pride ourselves on our cultural diversity, we have little self-knowledge. This paper will show the ways in which, for the outsider, these rights are under increasing threat. The result is a creeping demolition of public intention and social policy that employs euphemisms and avoids critique, leaving in its wake a slow painful decline of vulnerable communities.

This paper will draw from Rankin's 25 years' experience as director of BIGhART, a performance company based in Tasmania, to which innovation in form and structure, and a mission for better cultural understanding, is central. He reflects on the lessons learnt from their successes and failures; and places their body of work in an international context of alternative company practice.

BIGhART's renowned productions include *Ngapartji! Ngapartji!*, *Hipbone Sticking Out* and *The Namatjira Project.*